GETTING OUT OF DEBT

HOWARD L. DAYTON, JR.

POCKET GUIDES
Tyndale House Publishers, Inc.
Wheaton, Illinois

Quotes from the Bible, unless otherwise identified, are taken from
The Living Bible. Also cited are *The Amplified Bible (AMP), the
King James Version of The Holy Bible* (KJV), and *The New American
Standard Bible* (NASB).

Getting Out of Debt is adapted from *Your Money: Frustration or
Freedom?* by Howard L. Dayton, Jr. © 1982 by Howard L. Dayton,
Jr.

Second printing, June 1986
Library of Congress Catalog Card Number 85-52097
ISBN 0-8423-1004-5
© 1986 by Howard L. Dayton, Jr.
Printed in the United States of America

CONTENTS

The Credit Crunch

Allen and Jean Hitchcock have a problem.

Their debts total more than $9,000, not including a $37,500 house mortgage. They have two loans from a bank, one from a finance company, bills from three department stores, and $3,500 owed on an assortment of eleven credit cards.

The Hitchcocks' indebtedness started soon after they had married when they applied for their first loan. Jean, who grew up in a wealthy family, said, "Our friends had new cars, and we felt deprived. We had to have a new car, too."

Later, when they were transferred to Orlando, they impulsively bought a house in the suburbs, borrowing $3,000 from a bank for the down payment. They increased the bank loan to $3,500 when they began to fall behind on mortgage payments. The debts piled up. Jean said, "The man from the bank told us he was going to take our house and garnishee [take over] Allen's salary."

"Most of our debts were accumulated so slowly through the years," Allen said, "we didn't realize what was happening until it was too late."

BORROWING—A WAY OF LIFE

Each year millions of Americans find themselves in the Hitchcocks' predicament. In fact, the average American family spends $400 a year more than it earns.

Credit was once the exclusive privilege of the well-to-do, but the consumer picture has dramatically changed. The cash-on-the-barrelhead society has become the credit society, and Americans have responded by borrowing like never before—first for their home, then for their car and refrigerator, and finally for their pleasure.

Statistics prepared by the Federal Reserve show that consumer installment debt has multiplied more than thirty-one times since 1945. Personal debts have reached a point where it takes approximately one dollar out of every four that consumers earn (after taxes) to keep up the payments. Borrowing has become a way of life for most Americans.

CREDIT CASUALTIES

But "with so much credit around, you're bound to have casualties," Vern Countryman, a Harvard professor, explains. "It's just like auto accidents. If you're going to have all those cars, you're going to have accidents."

One out of every twenty families that takes out a loan to buy a new car or uses a credit card to purchase school clothes for the children will have trouble making payments. And for almost a half of a million Americans each year, the burden of debt is so great that they declare bankruptcy.

These statistics indicate that the American family is facing an unprecedented financial crisis. A recent survey showed that more than 50 percent of all divorces are caused by financial pressures in the home. For many, the better marriage vow would have been "till debt do us part!"

THE SOLUTION

Jesus talked a lot about money. Sixteen of the thirty-eight parables were concerned with how to handle money and possessions. Howard Hendricks notes that "Jesus Christ said more about money than [about] heaven or hell combined."

Jesus must have realized that managing money and possessions would be a problem for most people. He dealt with money matters because money matters.

This book will teach you biblical principles of handling your money and possessions. It is designed to give you practical steps to integrate these principles into your life—and discover lasting freedom from financial strain.

CREEPING CREDIT

Many families in debt get there so slowly that they do not realize it until it becomes an overwhelming problem. This chart shows how creeping credit sneaks up on a family that spends just $3.35 a day ($100 a month) more than it earns. Assume an average interest charge of 12 percent compounded monthly for ten years.

Year	Amount Overspent	Accumulated Interest	Ending Balance
1	$ 1,200	$ 70	$ 1,270
2	1,200	300	2,700
3	1,200	700	4,300
4	1,200	1,300	6,100
5	1,200	2,200	8,200
6	1,200	3,300	10,500
7	1,200	4,600	13,000
8	1,200	6,400	16,000
9	1,200	8,500	19,300
10	1,200	11,000	23,000
Total	$12,000	$11,000	$23,000

At the end of ten years the family that overspends $3.35 a day owes a total of $23,000! Interest charges alone amount to $230 a month.

Getting Out of Debt

It sounds so easy, so attractive. "Introducing: the best friend your checking account ever had." "Relax: now there's an easy solution to those nagging money problems." "Buy now: and pay later with a small monthly payment."

Have these credit card companies and banks finally come up with a quick, painless answer to your financial problems? No, they are merely presenting the positive, and temporary, aspects of instant credit. These solutions add up to one word which the advertisers neglect to mention: debt.

THE BIBLE ON DEBT

The Bible speaks point-blank to the subject of debt. "Keep out of debt and owe no man anything, except to love one another" (Rom. 13:8, AMP).

I like this translation because it reads like a road sign—KEEP OUT OF DEBT. Is there any wonder why it wasn't too many years ago that it was considered a sin for a

Christian to be in debt? The writer of Proverbs explains the reason God speaks so directly to the principle of staying out of debt. "Just as the rich rule the poor, so the borrower is servant to the lender" (Prov. 22:7).

When you are in debt you have lost a degree of your freedom, and the deeper you

---

☞ CHECKPOINT
Are You in Debt?

1. *Do you owe money with payments due?* If you purchased merchandise on a credit card with funds set aside to pay for the entire billing at the end of the month, then you are not in debt. However, if you are unable to pay the entire billing and carry a balance due, then you have qualified to be a member of the debt set!

2. *Does the amount owed (liability) on an item exceed its asset value?* For example, if you purchase a new car for $5,000 with $200 cash down and finance the remaining $4,800, then you are in debt because a car depreciates substantially the moment you drive it out of the showroom. Even if you sold the car, the cash proceeds would not be enough to cover the amount owed. This is true with almost any depreciating asset—furniture, clothes, and boats.

are in debt the more freedom you have lost. When payments drag on for months and years, when finance charges and interest rates eat away at your paychecks, when you are unable to give sacrificially to the church because you are paying sacrificially for your possessions, then you are in financial bondage to the lender.

The Bible clearly calls us to start getting out of debt as quickly as we can. "Evil men borrow and 'cannot pay it back'! But the good man returns what he owes with some extra besides" (Ps. 37:21). "Don't withhold repayment of your debts. Don't say 'some other time,' if you can pay now" (Prov. 3:27, 28). It is never easy, but it is God's desire for us to be free from the servitude of debt, and all things are possible with God.

HOW TO BEAT THE DEBT TRAP
Establish a written budget. A written budget is the first and most important step in getting out of debt because it is a plan for spending money. A three-part strategy is required in your spending habits:

1. Stop spending more than you make.
2. Pay the interest on the debt.
3. Repay the debt.

You can use a budget to schedule your debt reduction and to monitor progress. (See page 37.) A budget can also help you analyze your spending patterns to see where you can cut back, and it is an effective bridle on impulse spending.

Make a list of all your assets. List every asset you own: your home, car, furniture, cash, etc. See the Asset List for a guideline.

ASSET LIST—WHAT IS OWNED

1. Cash and Assets Easily Convertible to Cash
   - (a) Cash _____
   - (b) Stocks (market value) _____
   - (c) Bonds _____
   - (d) Cash value of life insurance (call agent) _____
   - (e) Coins _____
2. Real Estate
   - (a) Home (market value) _____
   - (b) Other real estate _____
3. Receivables
   - (a) Mortgage receivables _____
   - (b) Notes receivable _____
4. Other Investments _____
5. Automobiles (call dealer for today's value) _____
6. Personal Property*
   - (a) Furniture _____
   - (b) Boats _____
   - (c) Cameras _____
   - (d) Hobbies _____
   - (e) Other _____
7. Accrued Retirement Benefits _____
   Total Assets _____

*Personal property is the most difficult of assets to evaluate. Appraise as conservatively as possible because the depreciated value of second-hand personal property is ordinarily quite low.

Evaluate the completed list to determine whether you should sell any unnecessary assets to help you get out of debt more quickly.

Make a list of all your debts. Develop a clear picture of what you owe. List all of your debts (including those to relatives), with the monthly payment required and the annual rate of interest.

DEBT LIST—WHAT IS OWED

	Monthly Payment	Interest Rate	Balance Due
1. Home Mortgage	_____	_____	_____
2. Credit Card Companies	_____	_____	_____
3. Bank	_____	_____	_____
4. Installment Loans	_____	_____	_____
5. Loan Companies	_____	_____	_____
6. Insurance Companies	_____	_____	_____
7. Credit Union	_____	_____	_____
8. Loans from Relatives	_____	_____	_____
9. Other Personal Loans	_____	_____	_____
10. Business Loans	_____	_____	_____
11. Medical Loans	_____	_____	_____
12. Others	_____	_____	_____
Total Debts	══════	══════	══════

As you will discover from analyzing the interest rates on your debt list, credit costs vary greatly: from as little as 12 percent a year for a loan from a credit union or a bank, to 19 percent for credit cards, to 21 percent and up for installment purchases, to 22-30 percent from a finance or small-loan company.

The listing of your debts will assist you in establishing a priority for reducing your indebtedness. Try to retire the highest interest rate debts first.

Establish a repayment schedule. We all need a systematic written payment schedule to reach the goal of "D Day"—"debtless day."

A typical repayment schedule looks something like this:

REPAYMENT SCHEDULE

Creditor _____

	Monthly Payment	Months Remaining	Balance Due
January	_____	_____	_____
February	_____	_____	_____
March	_____	_____	_____
April	_____	_____	_____
May	_____	_____	_____
June	_____	_____	_____
July	_____	_____	_____
August	_____	_____	_____
September	_____	_____	_____
October	_____	_____	_____
November	_____	_____	_____
December	_____	_____	_____

After you have made your monthly payments, write down the amount paid and compute the balance due. Recording your payments will give you a sense of accomplishment, and watching the balance diminish will give you the incentive that will help you persist in your plan.

If you are deeply in debt or have been past due on your payments to creditors, it is a good idea to send them a copy of your repayment schedule. It is the rare creditor who will not go along with a person making a serious effort to systematically pay his debt. They will appreciate the fact that you have made out a schedule and have been concerned enough to share it with them.

As you pay off a creditor, begin to apply that payment to another debt to more quickly reduce your total indebtedness.

Apply additional income. Another way to expedite your freedom from debt is to agree in advance to apply any additional income to the repayment of debt. This includes such income as overtime pay, income tax refunds, garage sale earnings, odd jobs, payments, or any other income. Be sure that your extra money is applied to the reduction of debt and not to a higher level of spending.

Accumulate no new debts. A foolproof way to do this is to only pay for things with cash. Don't use credit cards. Somehow they give people the feeling that they're not spending real money—it's just "funny money." Like the shopper who said to a friend, "I like credit cards; they go so much farther than cash!" It has been proven that the family that uses credit cards will spend more money. Beware of plastic money!

15

Be content with what you have. The advertising industry has developed powerful and sophisticated tools largely aimed at creating discontentment in our lives. For example, advertising on television has a big impact on people because the average American watches television twenty hours a week. The average one-half hour of television viewing has thirteen commercials, which means that the average American watches between fifty and a hundred TV commercials a day. Advertising is designed for one purpose—to encourage us to buy something often by creating in us a lack of contentment with what we already have.

Four Axioms of Spending

1. The more shopping we do, the more we spend.
2. The more we watch television, the more we spend.
3. The more time we spend looking through catalogs, the more we spend.
4. The more we read magazines and newspaper advertisements, the more we spend.

It is much easier to remain content with what you have if you purposely avoid the temptations caused by advertising.

Do not give up! Recognize from the beginning there will be a hundred logical reasons to quit or delay your efforts to get out of debt.

Don't! Don't! Don't!

Don't stop until you have reached the marvelous goal of freedom from debt. Remember, getting out of debt is just plain hard work, but the rewards are worth the struggle.

WHEN TO BORROW MONEY

Scripture does not tell us whether we can legitimately borrow money for any specific assets or purposes, so this section is strictly my own opinion. Please critically examine this issue, then prayerfully reach your own conclusion.

I believe money should only be borrowed for three items*: (1) home, (2) business, (3) education.

I also believe that before you borrow for any of these items, three criteria should be met:

1. Borrowing should be limited to appreciating assets or assets that produce an income.

2. The value of the asset should equal or exceed the amount borrowed to acquire the item.

3. The amount borrowed should be

*Note: the automobile is not included in the list of items for which money can be borrowed. However, there are circumstances in which a person may borrow for an automobile. These are discussed in the chapter, "Questions and Answers."

within your ability to repay without placing a strain on your budget.

Let me illustrate how these criteria work in the purchase of a house. The family house has historically been an appreciating asset. It meets our first criterion. Second, if a house is purchased with a reasonable down payment, then its value will be greater than the mortgage. To meet the third criterion, the house purchased should not be so expensive that the monthly payments are too difficult to meet. If all three criteria are met, then in my opinion borrowing can be justified.

But be careful. Even if all the criteria are satisfied, the borrower still is a "servant" who is obligated to the lender. Meeting the criteria only improves your chances of repaying the debt. It is not a guarantee.

Society says: Buy now and pay later with those easy monthly payments.

Scripture says: "Keep out of debt" (Rom. 13:8).

Saving and Investing Your Money

"The average American family is three weeks away from bankruptcy," a recent article declared. "The average family has little or no money saved, a large amount of fixed monthly living expenses and credit obligations, and total dependence upon next month's income to remain solvent."

These statistics indicate that many people have not followed God's principles for saving. In fact, the United States has the lowest rate of saving among the wealthy countries of the world.

THE JOSEPH PRINCIPLE

Saving and investing are sometimes considered taboo subjects—something that spiritual people should avoid discussing. Many Christians seem to have the idea that to save means not to trust in God for his provision. This is not correct.

A skillful steward divides his income among sharing, spending, and saving. "The wise man saves for the future, but the foolish man spends whatever he gets" (Prov. 21:20).

An example is Joseph, the faithful steward, who saved from the seven years of plenty to insure that there would be food enough to eat during the seven years of famine.

I call saving the Joseph Principle. Saving means to forego an expenditure today so that you will have something to spend in the future. Perhaps this is why most people never save; it requires a denial of something that you want today, and our culture is not a culture of denial. Because it is a culture of instant gratification, most people spend their entire income.

Three Good Reasons to Save

1. Saving provides a cushion to meet the cost of unexpected events—loss of employment, major repairs, and sudden illness.
2. Savings should be accumulated to enable you to purchase your car, furniture, and other items of expense without having to use credit.
3. Accumulated savings provide a pool of resources for investing.

HOW TO START SAVING
Establish a habit of saving. Make yourself your number one creditor, after God, of

course. Consistently save a portion of your income, putting it into a savings account or savings program. The percentage of your income that you save does not matter. What is important is that you establish a pattern of regular savings.

To develop this habit you can use several different methods. You might set aside a certain percent of your income each month in a savings account. Or it might be easier for you to use one of the compulsory savings plans that are available through most banks, or an employee payroll plan. Here is a maxim for saving: *If the money budgeted for saving is deducted directly from your paycheck, you will save more.*

Review the incentives. As you begin to save, you will discover what bankers have known for a long time: the benefits of interest—money working for, not against, you.

How does money work for the saver? Assume a family saves $100 a month and receives 12 percent interest, compounded monthly. After twenty-five years, the family will earn $1900 each month in interest alone! What an incentive to begin saving.

For an even greater incentive to save, compare the results of spending $100 more than you earn each month with spending $100 less than you earn each month. Should you spend $100 more each month for ten years, you will owe $23,000; spend $100 less and you will own $23,000—a staggering difference of $46,000 at the end of ten years!

Begin now. The biggest enemy of saving is procrastination. For instance, if you plan to save $100 a month for twenty-five years at 12 percent interest, you will accumulate more than $189,800. However, look what happens if you decide to delay such a program by one year. Although you will have an extra $100 a month to spend for one year, it will cost you $22,500 in accumulated savings on the other end. Do not wait— begin to save now!

MONEY WORKING FOR YOU AT 12 PERCENT INTEREST

Year	Amount Saved	Accumulated Interest	Ending Balance
1	$ 1,200	$ 80	$ 1,280
2	1,200	300	2,700
3	1,200	800	4,400
4	1,200	1,400	6,200
5	1,200	2,200	8,200
6	1,200	3,400	10,600
7	1,200	4,800	13,200
8	1,200	6,600	16,400
9	1,200	8,700	19,500
10	1,200	11,200	23,200
10 year Subtotal	12,000	11,200	23,200
11-15	6,000	32,500	50,500
16-20	6,000	79,900	99,900
21-25	6,000	159,800	189,800
Total	$30,000	$159,800	$189,800

HOW TO START INVESTING

Investments differ from savings in that they are not always quickly convertible to cash, and they represent a conscious effort to provide for specific future events or build a hedge against inflation. For example, college for children and funding for retirement represent future expenditures that may be planned and financed from current income.

There is no investment without risk, and Scripture does not recommend any specific financial investments. I prefer to spread the risk by diversifying according to these priorities: (1) life insurance, (2) vocation, (3) house, and (4) other investments.

George Fooshee, in his excellent book *You Can Be Financially Free,* says:

> The first priority is life insurance because that's the only way for most of us to provide for our families in the event of our own death. . . .*
>
> Your vocation should rank next as an investment. Your own education is an investment that should pay excellent returns during your working years. One principle in Scripture is to invest in your business, which will be productive, then build your house: "Develop your business first before building your house" (Prov. 24:27). Many people today reverse this order. The large house, purchased early in life, tends to involve so much of their money that investing in their vocation is out of the question.

* The type of insurance you buy should depend upon your own analysis of the costs and benefits of each kind.

The home is the third priority. During the last few decades, the home has been one of the steadiest profitable investments for the average family.

Other investments (fourth priority) are almost as varied as the imagination. Real estate, oil, commodities, stocks, bonds, antiques, coins, and virtually anything people collect can be considered investments. Some of these, such as stocks, bonds, and real estate, pay a return on an annual basis. Others are held with the expectation that they will increase in value as time goes by.

Your investments beyond life insurance, vocation, and house should be matched with your own interests and personality. If you were raised on a farm and have knowledge of agricultural products and enjoy keeping abreast of the farm situation, then you might pursue a lifelong interest in agricultural investments. These could include everything from commodity purchases to owning and acquiring farmland. If common stocks are your interest, you might specialize in a study of those companies that are primarily agriculturally oriented.

All these investments that have been discussed are the kind that lend themselves to systematic investing. The regular monthly payment on the home for a twenty-year mortgage results in having a home completely paid for. . . . Steady hard work in your own business often results in a substantial salable asset. The key to most investments is to set aside regular amounts for systematic investing. "Steady plodding brings prosperity; hasty speculation brings poverty" (Prov. 21:5). [1]

THE DANGERS OF
SAVING AND INVESTING

As you are successful in accumulating your nest egg, it is easy to transfer your trust and affection from the invisible living God to your tangible assets. Money will certainly compete for your trust and attention. It has so much power that it is easy to be fooled into thinking that money provides our needs and our security. Money can become our first love. Paul warned Timothy of this temptation in 1 Timothy 6:10, 11: "For the love of money is the first step toward all kinds of sin. Some people have even turned away from God because of their love for it. . . . Run from all these evil things."

I would like to suggest a radical antidote for the potential disease of loving money: *Determine a maximum amount of savings and investments that you will accumulate and stop there.*

The amount will vary from individual to individual. If you are single without any dependents, the amount may be modest. If you have a family with educational needs, it may be more substantial. If you are the owner of a sizable business that requires large amounts of capital, the amount may be in the millions.

Each person should decide before God what amount will be his maximum. After you have reached your maximum goal, begin to share the portion of your income that used to be allocated to savings and investments.

☞ C H E C K P O I N T
Recognize a Risky Investment

To help you identify a potentially risky investment, ask yourself the following questions:

1. Is the prospect of a large profit "practically guaranteed"?
2. Does the decision to invest need to be made quickly, allowing you no opportunity to thoroughly investigate the investment or the promoter?
3. Does the promoter say he has an "excellent track record," and is doing you a "favor" by allowing you to invest with him?
4. Does the investment offer attractive tax deductions as an incentive?
5. Do you know little or nothing about the particular investment?
6. Is very little said about the risks of losing money?
7. Does the investment appear to require no effort on your part?
8. Are you promised a "handsome profit" quickly?

If you answered yes to one or more of these questions, you should be careful to thoroughly investigate the investment before risking your money. Seek the wise counsel of those experienced in that particular investment medium. And remember, be patient! I have never known anyone who made money in a hurry. Diligence, study, and counsel improve your chances for successful investments.

Society says: Spend all you make. However, if you should save, put your trust in your accumulated assets.

Scripture says: "The wise man saves for the future, but the foolish man spends whatever he gets" (Prov. 21:20).

Sharing Your Income

"I wonder if I'm obligated to give this week. . . . I gave $5 last week.

"I better put something in the plate, even if it's just a dollar. I wouldn't want that couple next to me to think I'm stingy."

"Well, at least this dollar is a tax deduction."

These unspoken reactions to a Sunday morning offering time reflect the frustration many people feel toward sharing. Often this frustration stems from a lack of understanding about the purposes and the practical how-to's of sharing.

THE BIBLE ON SHARING

Without apology the Old and New Testaments place a great deal of emphasis on giving.

In fact, more verses have to do with sharing than with any other subject on money. There are commands, practical suggestions, examples, and exhortations concerning this facet of stewardship. Everywhere in the Bible covetousness and greed are condemned, and generosity and charity are encouraged.

The major purpose of sharing is to benefit the giver. Jesus said, "It is more blessed to give than to receive" (Acts 20:35). It might be said that giving is not God's way of raising money, it's God's way of raising men.

Sharing develops our character. God understands that for us to develop into the people he wants us to be, we must learn how to share our possessions freely. If we don't, our inbred selfishness will grow and dominate us.

Sharing is the most effective antidote to the human disease of covetousness. "Instruct them . . . to be generous and ready to share . . . so that they may take hold of that which is life indeed" (1 Tim. 6:18, 19, NASB).

Sharing leads to contentment. A consistent habit of sharing is the best reminder that God is the sovereign owner of all we have been given to possess. As we share our money, we sharpen our focus on the part that God plays in finding true contentment.

Sharing trains our attention on the living God. "The purpose of tithing is to teach you always to put God first in your lives" (Deut. 14:23). An effective way of helping to visualize God's involvement in your sharing is to imagine that you are placing your gift into the nail-scarred hands of Jesus himself.

Sharing is an investment. Whatever we share on earth becomes an eternal investment accruing to our account. Jesus said, "Do not lay up for yourselves treasures upon earth, where moth and rust destroy, and where thieves break in and steal. But lay up for yourselves treasures in heaven, where neither moth nor rust destroys, and where thieves do not break in or steal" (Matt. 6:19, 20, NASB).

HOW TO SHARE SUCCESSFULLY

Set aside a tithe. Old Testament society was governed by a law that strictly set the minimum amount to be given—the tithe, or a tenth of a person's earnings. When the children of Israel disobeyed this commandment, it was regarded as robbing God himself (Mal. 3:8, 9). In addition to the tithe, the Hebrews were encouraged to give offerings that were voluntary.

The tithe is a simple and systematic method of sharing. However, it has a potential trap that I sometimes find myself falling into—treating the tithe as just another bill to be paid and not reflecting or praying about its use.

Give sacrificially. The New Testament builds on the foundation of the tithe and offering. The first addition is the instruction to give as God has prospered you. "On every Lord's Day each of you should put aside something from what you have earned during the week, and use it for this offering.

31

The amount depends on how much the Lord has helped you earn" (1 Cor. 16:2).

Second, the New Testament encourages sacrificial giving: "Now I want to tell you what God in his grace has done for the churches in Macedonia. Though they have been going through much trouble and hard times, they have mixed their wonderful joy with their deep poverty, and the result has been an overflowing of giving to others. They gave not only what they could afford, but far more" (2 Cor. 8:1-3).

Notice the great care taken to show that it was not in circumstances of prosperity that the Macedonians gave their liberal offering.

Give prayerfully. I believe that there is a reason Scripture is unclear about exactly how much we should share. The decision as to the amount an individual gives should be based on a personal relationship with God. As he seeks the guidance of the Spirit through an active prayer life, sharing suddenly becomes an exciting adventure.

After a great deal of thought and prayer, my wife and I have concluded that the tithe is the minimum amount we will share. Then, the more God prospers us, the greater percentage we should share from our income. I encourage you to prayerfully consider the amount God is calling you to share.

Share with your family. In the Bible, we are told to share with three categories of people. With whom and in what proportion one shares varies with the needs God lays on the heart of each believer.

In our culture we are experiencing a tragic breakdown in the area of sharing with family members. Husbands have failed to provide for their wives, parents have neglected their children, and grown sons and daughters have forsaken their elderly parents. Such neglect is solemnly condemned: "But if any one does not provide for his own, and especially for those of his household, he has denied the faith, and is worse than an unbeliever" (1 Tim. 5:8, NASB).

Share with Christian work and workers. Throughout its pages the Bible focuses on maintenance of the ministry. The Old Testament priesthood was to receive specific support (Num. 18:21), and the New Testament teaching on ministerial support is just as strong.

However, some have wrongly taught poverty for Christian workers. Thus many believe that those who are in various forms of Christian ministry should be poor. That position is not scriptural. "Pastors who do their work well should be paid well and should be highly appreciated, especially those who work hard at both preaching and teaching (1 Tim. 5:17).

How many Christian workers have been driven to distraction from their ministry by inadequate support? How many full-time Christian workers have had their dignity destroyed by having to accept handouts and "pastors' discounts" in order to make ends meet? God never intended his servants to exist at the level of bare subsistence. As someone has said, "The poor and starving pastor should exist only among poor and starving people."

Should all of your giving be done through your local church? In the case of my wife and I, the answer is no. A large portion of our giving supports our local church because we believe we should support the places that minister to our personal needs. The remainder of the support which we earmark for Christian work goes to ministries beyond our local church.

Share with the poor. Conservative estimates are that one billion people in the world go to bed hungry each night. That kind of statistic is awesome. It gives us the feeling that there is nothing we can do about such an immense problem.

Christians are instructed to give to the poor. It is an important teaching that is emphasized by the fact that the poor and the destitute are mentioned in the majority of those verses that discuss who should be the recipient of our sharing. "If you give to the poor, your needs will be supplied. But a curse upon those who close their eyes to poverty" (Prov. 28:27).

We must be diligent and creative in determining how we can most effectively identify the poor throughout our own country and the world. Then we must work to meet their needs.

Two Examples of Sharing

SUE

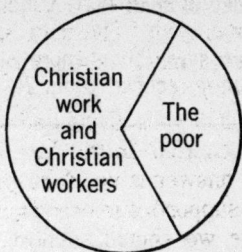

Sue is a single working woman. Her father supports Sue's mother and himself. Sue channels the bulk of her giving through her local church, but also shares a percentage of her income with the poor through gifts to a Christian relief and development organization and her church's benevolence fund.

BEN AND ELLEN

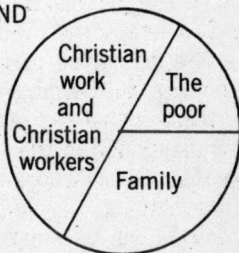

Ben and Ellen care for Ellen's aged mother in their home. In addition to helping cover her living expenses, they tithe to their church and help pay the salaries of a missionary couple in Brazil. Occasionally, they loan money to a struggling single-parent family without expecting repayment.

Society says: It is more blessed to receive than to give.

Scripture says: "It is more blessed to give than to receive" (Acts 20:35).

Budgeting Your Paycheck

Someone has said, "Expenses will always tend to rise just a little higher than income."

I have seen countless examples of this. Invariably, whether a family earns $8,000 or $80,000 a year, it probably will have too much month at the end of the money unless there is a carefully planned and disciplined approach to spending.

WHY BOTHER TO BUDGET?

Budgeting makes your money go further. When a family plans where its money is to go, it can make the money go further. That's what a budget is—a plan for spending money.

It is not always fun, but budgeting is the only way to meet basic needs and still apply what has been learned about getting out of debt, saving, and sharing. Regardless of the income, most families have difficulty making ends meet unless there is a plan for spending. Using a budget introduces an attitude of control in spending that is needed to reach financial objectives.

Budgeting creates family closeness. This is important because 48 percent of the most serious marital problems are financial, according to a recent survey of young husbands. In fact, one judge has said that quarreling about money is the major reason

MONTHLY BUDGET FORM

Income per Month

Salary   _____

Interest
  income   _____

Dividends   _____

Expenses per Month

1. Sharing	_____	(d) Mainte-	
2. Taxes		nance	_____
(a) Income		(e) Telephone	_____
taxes	_____	(f) Utilities	_____
(b) Social		(g) Other	_____
Security	_____	5. Food	
(c) Other		(a) Eating at	
taxes	_____	home	_____
3. Saving	_____	(b) Eating out	_____
4. Housing		6. Clothing	_____
(a) Payments	_____	7. Transportation	
(b) Insurance	_____	(a) Payments	_____
(c) Taxes	_____	(b) Gasoline	_____

---

for America's unprecedented divorce rate. Developing a budget together can eliminate many marital conflicts.

A successful budget should be a "team effort." Budgeting can help each member of the family participate in deciding what should be purchased and what the goals of the family should be.

Rental
  income _____

Other
  income _____

Total
Income ═══════

(c) Mainte- nance	_____	(d) Vacations	_____
(d) Other	_____	(e) Recreation	_____
8. Insurance		(f) Personal allowance	_____
(a) Auto- mobile	_____	(g) Other	_____
(b) Life	_____	10. Debt Reduction	
(c) Health	_____	(a) Credit card	_____
9. Miscellaneous	_____	(b) Installment	_____
(a) Medical/ Health	_____	(c) Other	_____
(b) Education	_____	Total	
(c) Gifts	_____	Expenses	═══════

HOW TO BUILD
A REALISTIC BUDGET

No one I have known to be in financial difficulty used a budget. Some had made a budget and then promptly filed it away. Others had made an unrealistic budget that provided nothing for such items as clothing or medical care. A budget is useful only if it is used. It should be a plan tailor-made for managing your finances, not someone else's.

To set up your budget, you need only a simple inexpensive notebook of accounting paper that can be bought in most bookstores. Then follow these three steps:

List your current expenses. Developing a realistic budget must begin with the current situation. Determine precisely how much money is earned and spent.

In my experience, spending tends to be significantly underestimated, particularly in

ANNUAL EXPENSE FORM 19—

Item	Jan	Feb	Mar	Apr	May	Jun
real estate taxes						
home owners' insurance						$225

the areas of food, clothing, transportation, and miscellaneous expenses. For this reason it is essential for you and your family to keep a strict accounting of every penny for a month to get an accurate picture of what you are actually spending.

The most efficient way to accomplish this is to pay for all large purchases by check. Then, have each family member carry a small notebook or a three-by-five card to record all cash purchases. In the evening record the check and cash purchases under the appropriate category on the Monthly Budget Form.

If your wages are not the same each month (for example, you are a commissioned salesman), make a conservative estimate of your annual income and divide by twelve to determine your monthly income.

Then complete the Annual Expense Form for those expenses that do not occur each

Jul	Aug	Sep	Oct	Nov	Dec

$300

month. Examples are real estate taxes and homeowner's insurance which are paid annually. Divide the yearly premium by twelve to arrive at the monthly expense. The Annual Expense Form will also be helpful in reminding you when to anticipate these periodic expenses.

Some expenses, such as vacations and auto repairs, do not come due every month. Estimate how much you spend for these on a yearly basis, divide that amount by twelve, and fill in the appropriate categories on the Monthly Budget Form.

Armed with this information you can construct an accurate budget of what you are actually spending and earning today. Do not be discouraged! Almost every budget I have seen starts out with expenditures in excess of income. But there is a solution.

Create an action plan. To solve the problem of spending more than you earn, you must either increase your income to the level of your expenditures or decrease your expenditures to the level of your income. It's that simple— either earn more or spend less. There are no other alternatives.

A part-time job, or better yet, a project that would involve the whole family, is a way of increasing your income. The ever-present danger of increasing income is the tendency for expenses also to rise. The key to eliminating this problem is to agree ahead of time to apply any extra income to balancing the budget.

Another potential problem in seeking to earn extra money is the sacrifice of strong family relationships.

To reduce spending, begin by asking some crucial questions about your personal budget. Which expenses are absolutely necessary? Which can I do without? Which can I reduce?

Here are some guidelines to help you evaluate your major expenses. When you exceed the upper range in any category, this should warn you to carefully evaluate your expenditures.

MAJOR EXPENSES

Category	Percent of Income (after sharing and taxes)
Shelter	20-35
Food	15-25
Transportation	10-15
Clothing	4-8
Insurance	3-5
Health	3-5
Entertainment and Recreation	3-5
Debts	0-10
Saving	5-10
Miscellaneous	3-5

The best way to reduce spending is to plan ahead. Decide in advance what you need and make a list. By using the "need list," you will be able to shop more wisely and avoid impulse spending. Use the money-saving tips listed on page 71 to help you lower your expenses.

Do not stop! The most common temptation is to stop budgeting. Don't do it!

Remember, a budget is simply a plan for spending your money. It will not work by itself. Every area of your budget should be regularly reviewed to keep a rein on spending. "Any enterprise is built by wise planning, becomes strong through common sense, and profits wonderfully by keeping abreast of the facts" (Prov. 24:3, 4).

To help us "keep abreast of the facts," at the middle of each month my family compares our actual income and expenses with the amounts budgeted. If we find ourselves overspending, we make mid-month adjustments by cutting back on our spending plans for the rest of the month. You need to maintain adequate records to compare the money actually spent with your budget.

Through the years there will be frustrations, but a budget, if properly used, will save you thousands of dollars. It will help you accumulate the savings for your children's education and your retirement. It will help you stay out of debt. More important, it will help the husband and wife communicate together in an area that is a leading cause of marital conflict.

Five Budgeting Hints

1. *Reconcile your checkbook each month.*

2. *Keep a special savings account* in which to put aside the monthly allotment for the bills that do not come due each month. For example, if your annual insurance premium is $240, each month deposit twenty dollars in this savings account. This method will insure that the money will be available when these payments come due.

3. *Measure expenses in terms of their yearly cost.* For example, if you spend $2.50 for lunch each working day, multiply $2.50 by five days a week by fifty-two weeks a year. It totals $650 for lunches. This will help you give proper attention to seemingly inconsequential expenses.

4. *Control impulse-spending.* Each time you have the urge to spend for something not planned, post it to an "impulse list" and date it. Then wait thirty days and pray about buying the item. If you're like me, I guarantee that you will not purchase at least half of the items, because impulses do not last.

5. *Include personal allowances in the budget.* Each should be given an allowance to spend as he or she pleases. The wife can go to the beauty shop and the husband can play golf as often as they like, so long as the allowance holds out. This will eliminate many arguments.

Society says: Spend what you will and let the chips fall where they may.

Scripture says: "Any enterprise is built by wise planning" (Prov. 24:3).

Setting New Goals

Most Americans believe you can buy happiness. The American Institute of Public Opinion recently found that 70 percent of Americans thought they would be happier if they could earn only $37 more a week. I find myself periodically siding with this majority—falling into the "if only" trap.

"If only" I had a new car, I would be satisfied. "If only" I lived in that nice house, I would be content. "If only" I had his job, I would be happy. The list is endless.

THE BIBLE ON WEALTH
The Bible offers a sharp contrast to the attitude of the materialist.

Money will not bring true happiness in life. "Solomon, the author of Ecclesiastes, had an annual income of more than $25 million. He lived in a palace that took thirteen years to build. He owned 40,000 stalls of horses. He sat on an ivory throne overlaid with gold.

47

He drank from gold cups. The daily menu of his household included a hundred sheep and thirty oxen in addition to fallow-deer and fatted fowl."[2]

Obviously, Solomon was in a position to know whether money would bring happiness, and he did not hesitate to say that riches do not bring true happiness: "He who loves money shall never have enough. The foolishness of thinking that wealth brings happiness! The more you have, the more you spend, right up to the limits of your income" (Eccl. 5:10, 11).

Wealth is morally neutral, but dangerous. Many have misquoted 1 Timothy 6:10 to read that "money is the root of all evil." But money can be used for good or for evil. It can build hospitals and schools as well as finance hard drugs and war.

The root of all evil is in the mind of man, not his money. Sinfulness is determined by attitude, not affluence. Wealth will not corrupt a man if he has the proper perspective of it.

Nevertheless, hundreds of verses in Scripture warn of the dangers of wealth. God wanted to make us aware of the ease with which we can trust in tangible wealth rather than Him.

Jesus warned, "No servant can serve two masters; for either he will hate the one, and love the other, or else he will hold to one, and despise the other. You cannot serve God and riches" (Luke 16:13, NASB).

Haddon W. Robinson observes,

Serving money is very abstract. My house, my car, my investments do not mean more to me than God. But Jesus did not say that we must serve God more than money. Evaluating our lives to discover what occupies first place is not the proper test. The question is whether we serve money at all.

Either we serve God and use money or we serve money and use God. Yet, few Christians deliberately dedicate their lives to materialism. Wealth is deceitful, Jesus told us, and its bondage is subtle. Like the flypaper and the fly, the fly lands on the sticky substance thinking "my flypaper" only to discover that the flypaper says "my fly."[3]

I have wrestled with this during my business career. I was caught up in the excitement of building a new business and unwittingly began to evaluate people in terms of what they could do for me—not their worth as people.

I found myself thinking more highly of those who were wealthy or in a position to help me. However, I was confronted with my attitude when I read James 2:4: "Judging a man by his wealth shows that you are guided by the wrong motives." Without realizing it, I had been caught by the deceitfulness of wealth. To avoid this trap, we need to consistently evaluate our motives in light of Scripture.

The mark of the successful person is faithfulness. Usually the more wealth a person has accumulated, the more he has been thought to "succeed." The more expensive the home, the car, and the clothes, the more successful he is considered to be. Such an attitude is evidence that we think our success is related to how much we have.

However, according to Scripture it is impossible to tell if a person is truly successful by looking at his external circumstances, his possessions, or his position. If we had seen Joseph or Paul in prison, Daniel in the lions' den, or Job in his affliction and poverty—men who had lost everything—how many of us would have considered them successful?

☞ CHECKPOINT
What's Your Attitude Toward Money?

1. Am I willing to sacrifice my family, reputation, clear conscience, and relationship with God or other people in order to acquire money?
2. Do I think more highly of people who are wealthy?
3. Am I critical of people who are wealthy?
4. What worries me?
5. What do I think about when my mind goes into neutral?
6. Do I trust in my money to do what only God can do?
7. Do I think "if only" I had more money, a larger home, a newer car, or a better job, then I would be happy?

Webster's definition of success is "the degree or measure of attaining a desired end." And according to Scripture, the desired end for us is to become faithful stewards.

TWO KEYS TO CONTENTMENT

God's part. The Bible teaches that we can learn to be content in poverty as well as prosperity. "Not that I was ever in need, for I have learned how to get along happily whether I have much or little. I know how to live on almost nothing or with everything. I have learned the secret of contentment in every situation, whether it be a full stomach or hunger, plenty or want" (Phil. 4:11, 12).

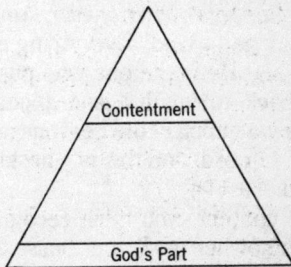

THE PYRAMID OF CONTENTMENT

The foundation of our contentment is knowing the part that the living God plays in our finances. *He has promised to provide our needs.* "All mankind scratches for its daily bread, but your heavenly Father knows your needs. He will always give you all you need from day to day (Luke 12:30, 31).

In 1 Timothy 6:8, God tells us what our needs are—food and covering. In other words, there is a difference between needs and wants. A need is a basic necessity of life—food, clothing, or shelter. A want is anything more than a need. A steak dinner, a new car, and the latest fashions—they are all wants.

God has obligated himself to provide our needs, but he has not promised to provide our wants. This is the heart of contentment—on one hand God promises to provide our needs, and on the other tells us to be content when these needs are met. "And if we have food and covering, with these we shall be content" (1 Tim. 6:8, NASB).

God is the sole owner of everything. "The earth belongs to God! Everything in all the world is his! He is the one who pushed the oceans back to let dry land appear" (Ps. 24:1). "Everything in the heavens and earth is yours, O Lord, and this is your kingdom" (1 Chron. 29:11).

To be content, you must recognize that God is the owner of all your possessions. If you believe you own even a single possession, then the circumstances that affect that possession will be reflected in your attitude. If something favorable happens to the possession, then you will be happy; but if something bad occurs, you will be discontent.

The issue in Scripture is how to handle faithfully all God has entrusted to us. The faithful steward is responsible for what he has, whether he has much or little. He can be wasteful and negligent whether he is poor or wealthy. In the 25th chapter of Matthew, God required good stewardship of the man who was given two talents as well as the man who was given five.

The faithful use of money leads to contentment. In Philippians we discover that Paul has learned to be content because: (1) he knew that God would supply all his needs (Phil. 4:19), and (2) he had been a faithful steward. "The things you have learned and received and heard and *seen in me*, practice these things" (Phil. 4:9, NASB).

The Bible offers contentment, and in the process it suggests real solutions to the financial problems of the twentieth century.

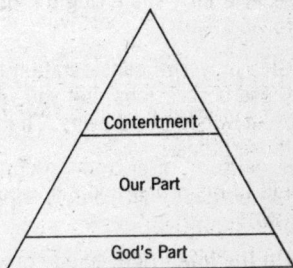

THE PYRAMID OF CONTENTMENT

Your part. What is the second key to contentment? To know—and do—what God requires of a good and faithful steward.

The word *steward* can be translated into three different words: manager, supervisor,

Deeding Your Assets to God

We all occasionally forget that God owns everything. We act as if we do.

A deed is often used to transfer the ownership of property. By completing and signing the following deed, you can acknowledge that God is the owner of your assets.

To complete the deed:

1. Print your name. You are the grantor, the one transferring ownership.

2. Write your home address.

3. We have already printed, "The Lord our God." (He is the one receiving the assets.)

4. Write *contentment*. That is what we receive for transferring the property to God.

5. Give prayerful consideration to those possessions that you wish to acknowledge God owns. Then list these items.

6. Fill in *his* or *her* and sign your name.

7. On the lower right-hand corner there is a space for the signature of two witnesses. These friends can help hold you accountable in a practical way for recognizing God as owner of your possessions.

DEED

This Deed made the _____day of _____,
A.D. 19_____,
(1)by,_____
(1) hereinafter called the grantor,
(2) whose address is _____
(3)to the grantee: The Lord our God.

(4) Witnesseth: That the grantor, for
and in consideration of _____
_____and other valuable consid-
erations, receipt whereof is hereby ac-
knowledged, hereby releases, conveys,
and confirms unto the grantee, all that
certain (5) _____
_____
_____
_____

In Witness Whereof, the said grantor
has hereunto set (6) _____hand and
seal the day and year first above written.
(6) _____

Signed, sealed, and delivered in our
presence:
To have and to hold, the same in fee
simple forever.
    (7)_____
    (7)_____

and overseer. In Scripture the position of a steward is one of great responsibility. He is the supreme authority under his master and has full responsibility for all his master's possessions and household affairs, even the raising of children.

As we examine Scripture we see that God, as Master, has given us the authority to be stewards. "You [God] have put him [man] in charge of everything you made; everything is put under his authority" (Ps. 8:6). Our only responsibility is to be faithful. "Moreover it is required in stewards, that a man be found faithful" (1 Cor. 4:2, KJV).

As Christians we have been taught much about giving, but little about how to faithfully handle all our money. However, God is not only concerned with the amount we give, but also with what we do with our entire income. In fact, he is interested in all that we have. By giving a small percentage, many Christians feel that they can bypass all other responsibilities and do as they please with the remainder of their money.

Society says: You will find happiness and peace as you accumulate enough wealth to support your desired standard of living.

Scripture says: You can be content in every circumstance as you follow the scriptural principles of how to handle your money and possessions.

Questions and Answers

Is a depression coming soon? If so, how should a person prepare to survive?

I am not an economic forecaster and do not know what the economy will be like in five years. However, America and most of the nations of the world are violating scriptural principles of handling money—particularly in the areas of debt and giving. And I believe that you cannot continue to violate a scriptural principle without suffering the consequences. I do not know if it will happen next week or twenty years from now, but if we do not stop violating Scripture, we will definitely pay the price.

The only way for us to prepare for economic chaos is by being faithful stewards: Eliminate all debt, become excellent in our work, establish a program of saving and investing, share liberally, and then trust God for his provision—even in a depression.

I am convinced that if we should go through an economic depression, the faithful, contented steward will stand out from the crowd that has built its happiness on favorable circumstances. It should be a fantastic opportunity to share the hope that is within us.

What is the Christian perspective on paying taxes?

This is an excellent example of the contrast between society and Scripture. Avoid paying taxes at any cost, our culture says; after all, the government wastes money at every turn—fat cats in Washington, welfare fraud, the bureaucrats, etc.

Entire financial industries are built around the practice of avoiding taxes. I have seen many investments that were sold, not because they made sound economic sense, but because they were advertised as "tax shelters."

There is a very fine line between tax avoidance and tax evasion, and there is a strong temptation to misappropriate funds that are legally due our government. An estimated $50 billion a year in taxes is lost in tax evasion.

I am not condoning the waste and excesses found in government. In fact, I believe a citizen should make an effort to influence government to be more efficient and responsive. But the Bible tells us of an additional responsibility: pay your taxes gladly!

"Obey the laws, then, for two reasons: first, to keep from being punished, and second, just because you know you should. Pay your taxes too, for these same two reasons. For government workers need to be paid so that they can keep on doing God's work, serving you. Pay everyone whatever he ought to have: pay your taxes and import duties gladly" (Rom. 13:5-7).

We have so much to be thankful for in America. The government provides many services we take for granted—highways, fire protection, potable water, etc. So pay your taxes gladly—this has revolutionized my attitude and I have a renewed sense of contentment around tax time when many are quite discontent.

Should I borrow to buy an automobile?

If possible, pay cash for your car. However, most people simply do not have the cash to acquire a car without borrowing. The car is a major purchase and approximately two out of three borrow to buy their car.

If you must borrow, I have three suggestions:

1. Shop for the best deal in financing your car. In general, the most expensive sources of automobile credit are the car dealers and finance companies. Credit unions and commercial banks are usually the least expensive.

2. Pray that God would provide a good, inexpensive used car to minimize your borrowing, or better yet to allow you to pay cash.

Last year it was necessary for Bev and me to get a second vehicle. We listed our requirements: a small pickup truck, in good mechanical condition, at a price of less than $500. We then prayed.

After three months a neighbor learned of our search. He owned a low mileage Datsun pickup in reasonable condition. He needed the truck once a month, but could no longer afford the insurance.

We bought the truck with the understanding that he could drive it the one day a month it was needed. The cost—$100! I firmly believe that we can experience the reality of God by praying about our spending decisions, and waiting to see his active involvement in meeting our needs.

3. Begin saving the money to buy your next car.

By purchasing the low-cost used truck, we have been able to save the amount that would have been going toward car payments. Each month we put the "car payment" in a separate savings account to accumulate enough cash to pay for our next car.

This is only one of many methods you can use to save. The key you can use to break the car financing habit is to begin saving now for your next car.

Should wives work?

That question is a paradox. All wives work—whether they are homemakers or work outside the home. A Stanford University study shows that wives who work outside the home carry a particularly heavy load of seventy to eighty hours a week with the responsibilities of their job plus homework.

The trend for wives to hold jobs is escalating rapidly. In 1947, working husbands outnumbered working wives five to one; now the ratio is less than two to one. For many reasons, women are becoming involved in jobs of all kinds. Wives work to provide additional income for their families and to express their creativity; and widows and divorcees work to provide for the needs of their families.

When young children are at home in their formative years, it is wise for a mother to remain at home, working only in extreme circumstances. "These older women must train the younger women to live quietly, to love their husbands and their children, and to be sensible and clean minded, spending their time in their own homes" (Titus 2:4, 5).

Proverbs 31 paints a beautiful picture of the working wife living a balanced life with the thrust of her activity toward the home. My opinion is that woman's work is not so much in the home as it is for the home. Proverbs 31 does not say that a wife should be confined to four walls, but involved in activities that relate to the home. I believe there are three broad justifications for a wife working outside the home:

1. When her salary helps to provide for family needs. Many times when the husband is in college, the wife works to provide the family's needs.

2. When professional talents or spiritual gifts are evident and no children are at home.

3. When the creativity and resourcefulness of a wife's hobbies and talents allow the family to be involved and not forsaken.

Should a Christian declare bankruptcy?

In the 1970s five of the ten largest bankruptcies in the history of American business occurred, capped by the collapse of the W. T. Grant retail chain. Bankruptcy knocks on the doors of individuals who earn as little as $100 a week, as well as multi-million dollar corporations. Indeed, there are nine times as many personal bankruptcies as there are corporate bankruptcies. In fact, personal bankruptcies now approach 250,000 a year.

Although the stigma of bankruptcy has rapidly diminished in recent years, I believe Scripture teaches that bankruptcy is not the normal way of getting out of debt. "Evil men borrow and 'cannot pay it back'! But the good man returns what he owes with some extra besides" (Ps. 37:21).

The Bible teaches that you should repay your debts. This has to be balanced. If you were an owner (a stockholder) of W. T. Grant, you might have some difficulty in paying Grant's $1 billion of indebtedness.

As a rule of thumb for determining your responsibilities for debt repayment: If you were intimately involved in the accumulation of the debts, you should intend to pay them back; if you were not actively involved, such as a stockholder in W. T. Grant, you probably are not responsible for their repayment.

Once responsibility is determined, make every effort to establish a schedule of repayment with your creditors and then adhere to the schedule.

I know of couples who have been forced into bankruptcy by unreasonable creditors. But once again, the only responsibility of a faithful steward is to do our part. And our part is to diligently try to pay back debts, to try to avoid bankruptcy, and to recognize that God's part is to control the circumstances surrounding a potential bankruptcy.

Should Christians expect to prosper?

John Wesley is quoted as saying, "True religion (a personal relationship with Jesus Christ) will result in the people of a nation becoming more hard working, honest, frugal, and thrifty, which results in the creation of wealth."

I think Wesley is correct. Christians who follow the principles of a faithful steward should expect to prosper. However, there are four reasons they may not.

1. *God wants to develop our character.* Joseph is an illustration of how God devel-

oped character in a man's life by taking away his prosperity. Although he had been faithful, Joseph went through some difficult situations, losing all he had as God built his character to prepare him to eventually be elevated to number-two man in the kingdom of Egypt. "We also exult in our tribulations, knowing that tribulation brings about perseverance; and perseverance, proven character" (Rom. 5:3, 4, NASB).

2. *God needs to discipline us.* In the Old Testament there were a number of times when God took away the wealth of the nation of Israel to discipline them and bring them back to himself. Similarly, in the New Testament John told his friend Gaius, "I pray that in all respects you may prosper . . . just as your soul prospers" (3 John 2, NASB).

I believe that God will lovingly withhold prosperity if it will bring us closer to him. It has been interesting the last several years to watch how a number of people in our community have changed their values as a result of the recession we had in the mid-1970s. As they lost their wealth, it gave them the motivation to question what really is important in life and turn to God.

3. *Nothing is certain in life.* Bill Stephens, a local residential real estate broker and a good friend of mine, is a hard-working professional who has made excellence his goal. I asked him what was the most important lesson God had taught him through his work. He replied with respect in his

voice, "Nothing in this life is certain except the Lord and his Word."

He then explained that the purchase of a home is usually the major purchase a person will make, and often emotions run high.

"I am compensated only if the sale is consummated," he said, "and I have learned the hard way that there is no such thing as a sure sale. But it is precisely this constant uncertainty in my business, coupled with the realization that God controls the circumstances, that has made me a more relaxed and contented person in all areas of life."

4. *God may choose not to prosper us.* Daniel and Jeremiah were two prophets who lived during the period of the Babylonian captivity. Each had a dramatically different economic status.

Daniel was prime minister of the Babylonian Empire. He must have lived in a fine home staffed with servants, earned a handsome salary, and had the finest "Cadillac chariot"—and Daniel was a faithful man.

Jeremiah was poor. He was repeatedly imprisoned, ridiculed, and impoverished. Yet, he also was a faithful man.

These faithful men were each at a different end of the economic spectrum. God in his infinite wisdom and mercy sovereignly chooses which of his faithful people he will prosper.

Should a Christian carry insurance?

The basic purpose of insurance is to

spread the risk of loss. Let's examine three types of insurance.

1. Self-insurance—a refusal to pay premiums to an insurance company to spread the risk of loss from sickness, casualty, or loss of life. The person hopes to meet contingencies out of personal reserves or subsequent provision.

2. Purchased insurance—payment of premiums to an insurance company to spread various risks of loss.

3. Faith insurance—to trust in other Christians or divine intervention, to make provision in the event of loss.

Frequently state laws or contracts provide for insurance requirements. We are to be subject to governmental authorities and keep our contractual promises. Responsibilities to creditors and family frequently demand that we carry insurance.

To purchase insurance does not mean we have a lack of faith.

The concept of "100-percent ownership by God" might lead one to self insurance, but the concept of "100 percent stewardship" probably leads toward purchased insurance.

Should I lend money to someone in need?

God's economy demands that we approach lending to individuals in need in a manner that is contrary to the practice of our culture. In the Old Testament we read that loans to needy fellow-Jews were to be interest-free.

And in the New Testament, not only was the loan to be interest-free, but the lender was not to expect repayment. "And if you lend money only to those who can repay you, what good is that? . . .Don't be concerned about the fact that they won't repay" (Luke 6:34, 35).

I want to stress that the interest-free loans that do not require repayment are to be for someone's needs—his food, clothing, or shelter. In my opinion, a loan for a person's wants can be interest-bearing with repayment expected.

From the lender's standpoint there is no difference between giving to someone in need and lending to his need. In both cases he earns no interest and does not expect repayment. But the recipient's position has changed. A gift requires no repayment, but a loan requires repayment. "Evil men borrow and 'cannot pay it back'! But the good man returns what he owes with some extra besides" (Ps. 37:21).

When someone comes seeking money, how do you know whether to consider giving it or lending it? Matthew 5:42 (NASB) tells us, "Give to him who asks of you, and do not turn away from him who wants to borrow from you." You let the person seeking funds tell you whether he wants a loan or a gift.

Let me give you an example of lending to

cement this issue for you. Two years ago a friend, Kyle Jackson, came to me asking for a loan for a personal need. His request qualified as a need, a basic necessity of life. I told my wife about the request, we prayed about it, and loaned him the money. As far as I was concerned, the money was Kyle's and I never expected repayment. We could continue our relationship without any feelings of guilt or strain if for some reason Kyle was unable to pay back the loan. After six months Kyle asked me out for lunch (which was the "extra besides") and repaid the loan.

Some time later Kyle came and asked for a gift because of a ministry in which he was involved. After I prayed with my wife, we gave him the money. My position had not changed. I still did not expect repayment, but his position had changed.

He is under no obligation before God to repay the gift.

Should you leave an inheritance for your children?

Yes. "When a good man dies, he leaves an inheritance" (Prov. 13:22).

You should provide an inheritance for your spouse and children. However, it probably is not wise to leave your children with great wealth if they have not been thoroughly schooled in the biblical perspective of money and how to properly manage it. "The almighty dollar bequeathed to a child is an almighty curse," Andrew Carnegie once said. "No man has the right to handicap his son with such a burden as great wealth. He must face this question squarely: Will the fortune be safe with my boy and will my boy be safe with my fortune?"

"An inheritance gained hurriedly in the beginning, will not be blessed in the end" (Prov. 20:21). The youth who has been trained to be a skillful steward of possessions is a rarity today.

In my opinion you should make provision for distributing an inheritance spread over several years or until the heir is mature enough to handle the responsibility of money. A good idea is to periodically test your children by giving them a small amount of money to see how wisely they use it. If they prove faithful with that small amount, they will be faithful with larger amounts.

Incidentally, seven out of ten of the 1.9 million Americans who died during 1976 did not have a will. To die intestate, without a will, is expensive and time-consuming and can be heartbreaking for your loved ones. It can literally destroy an estate left to provide for the family.

Scripture teaches that we brought nothing into the world and we will take nothing with us when we die. But we can leave it behind precisely as we wish—we can specify to whom and how much. If you die without a will, these decisions are left up to the court. Under some circumstances the court can appoint a guardian (who may not know the Lord) to raise your children if you have not made this provision in your will.

Whether you are married, single, rich or poor, you should have a will. Not only does it clear up any legal uncertainties, it also helps you map out your finances while you are alive so that you can protect the best interests of those whom you want to inherit your property.

Money-saving Tips

SHELTER

1. Purchase an older house that you can improve with your own labor, or buy a modest-size house suitable to your needs today with a design that can be expanded should you need more space in the future.

2. Consider living in an apartment. It is less expensive and has fewer responsibilities than a house—lawn care, maintenance, and so forth.

3. If you can do repair and maintenance work such as lawn spraying, pest control, painting, and carpet cleaning, you will save a substantial amount.

4. Lower the cost of utilities by limiting the use of heating, air conditioning, lights, and appliances.

5. Shop carefully for furniture and appliances. Garage sales are a good source for reasonably priced household goods.

FOOD

1. Prepare a menu for the week. Then list the ingredients from the menu and shop according to the list. This will help you plan a nutritionally balanced diet. Avoid impulse shopping, and eliminate waste.

2. Shop once a week. Each time we go shopping for "some little thing," we always buy "some other little thing" as well.

3. Cut out the ready-to-eat food which has expensive labor added to the price.

4. Leave children and hungry husbands home. The fewer distractions from the list the better.

5. The husband's lunches are often budget breakers. A lunch prepared at home and taken to work will help the budget and the waistline.

6. Reduce the use of paper products—paper plates, cups, and napkins are expensive to use.

TRANSPORTATION

1. If it is possible to get by with one car, this will be the biggest transportation savings.

2. Purchase a low-cost used car and drive it until repairs become too expensive.

3. The smaller the car, the more economical to operate. You pay an estimated thirty-five cents a pound each year to operate an automobile.

4. Perform routine maintenance yourself—oil changes, lubrication, etc. Regular

maintenance will prolong the life of your car.

5. If purchasing a new car, wait until new models are introduced in September. You can save 5 to 35 percent during these year-end sales.

CLOTHING

1. Make a written list of yearly clothing needs. Shop from the list during the off-season sales, at economical clothing stores, and at garage sales.

2. A wife who uses a sewing machine can cut the cost of garments in half.

3. Purchase simple basic fashions that stay in style longer than faddish clothes.

4. Do not purchase a lot of clothing. Select one or two basic colors for your wardrobe, and buy outfits that you can wear in combination with others.

5. Purchase home-washable fabrics. Clothes that must be commercially cleaned are expensive to maintain.

INSURANCE

1. Select insurance based on your need and budget, and secure estimates from three major insurance companies.

2. Exercising the deductible feature will substantially reduce premiums.

3. Seek the recommendation of friends for a skilled insurance agent. A good agent can save you money.

HEALTH

1. Practice preventive medicine. Your body will stay healthier when you get the proper amount of sleep, exercise, and nutrition.

2. Also practice proper oral hygiene to keep teeth healthy and to reduce dental bills.

3. Obtain the recommendation of friends for reasonable and competent physicians and dentists.

ENTERTAINMENT AND RECREATION

1. Time your vacation for the off season and select destinations near home.

2. Rather than expensive entertainment, seek creative alternatives such as family picnics or free state parks.

NOTES

1. George Fooshee, *You Can Be Financially Free* (Old Tappan, NJ: Revell, 1976), pp. 78-80.

2. Leslie B. Flynn, *Your God and Your Gold* (Grand Rapids, MI: Zondervan, 1961), p. 112.

3. Haddon Robinson, "Testimony of a Checkbook," *Christian Medical Society Journal* (1976), p. 3.

About the Author

HOWARD L. DAYTON, JR., a graduate of Cornell University, is the owner of a real estate development company. He has conducted seminars and lectured in the area of personal finance since 1974. Dayton and his wife, Bev, live in Orlando, Florida, with their children, Matthew and Danielle.

POCKET GUIDES
NEW FROM TYNDALE

■ *Hi-Fidelity Marriage* by J. Allen Petersen. respected family counselor shows you how to start an affair—with your own spouse. Learn how to keep love alive . . . rekindle old flames . . . grow from mistakes. You have what it takes to make your marriage better.

■ *Increase Your Personality Power* by Tim LaHaye. Why do you get angry? Afraid? Worried? Discover your unique personality type, then use it to live more effectively—at home, on the job, and under pressure. An easy-to-use format includes personality tests to take on your own.

■ *The Perfect Way to Lose Weight* by Charles T. Kuntzleman and Daniel V. Runyon. Anyone can lose fat—and keep it off permanently. This tested program, developed by a leading physical fitness expert, shows how. Helpful charts and safety tips round out this practical fat-loss plan.

■ *Strange Cults in America* by Bob Larson. An easy-reading update of six well-known cults: the Unification Church, Scientology, The Way International, Rajneesh, Children of God, and Transcendental Meditation. Includes special features on how to identify a cult and talk to a cult member.

■ *Temper Your Child's Tantrums* by Dr. James Dobson. You don't need to feel frustrated as a parent. The celebrated author and "Focus on the Family" radio host wants to give you the keys to firm, but loving, discipline in your home. Follow his proven counsel and watch the difference in your children.